Cover illustration: Kenrokuen garden, Ishikawa

Enman'in shrine, Shiga

Next page: Jizoin shrine, Mie

無限の空間

Infinite Spaces

The Art and Wisdom of the Japanese Garden

Edited by Joe Earle
Introduction by Julie Moir Messervy
Photographs by Sadao Hibi

Based on the *Sakuteiki* by Tachibana no Toshitsuna

TUTTLE PUBLISHING
Boston • Rutland, Vermont • Tokyo

Kenrokuen garden, Ishikawa

This edition first published in 2000 by Tuttle Publishing, an imprint of Periplus Editions (HK) Ltd, with editorial offices at 153 Milk Street, Boston, Massachusetts 02109.

Portions of Julie Moir Messervy's introduction first appeared in *Tenshin-en* published by MFA Publications, Boston.

Library of Congress Card Number: 00-102151
ISBN 0-8048-3259-5

Distributed by

North America, Latin America & Europe
Tuttle Publishing
Airport Business Park
364 Innovation Drive
North Clarendon, VT 05759-9436, USA
Tel: (802) 773 8930
Fax: (802) 773 6993
Email: info@tuttlepublishing.com
www.tuttlepublishing.com

Asia Pacific
Berkeley Books Pte Ltd
130 Joo Seng Road #06-01/03
Singapore 368357
Tel: (65) 6280 1330
Fax: (65) 6280 6290
Email: inquiries@periplus.com.sg
www.periplus.com

Japan
Tuttle Publishing
Yaekari Building, 3F
5-4-12 Osaki, Shinagawa-ku
Tokyo 141 0032, Japan
Tel: (03) 5437 0171
Fax: (03) 5437 0755
Email: tuttle-sales@gol.com

First edition
08 07 06 05 04   10 9 8 7 6 5 4 3

Designed by Lorraine Brown at Redback, Cambridge, UK

Printed in Singapore

Contents

Introduction

Julie Moir Messervy

With the publication of this beautiful book, one of the earliest treasures of Japanese garden design is at last available to the Western gardener. *Infinite Spaces* combines two remarkable elements: the secret teachings preserved in Tachibana no Toshitsuna's *Sakuteiki* [Notes on Garden Design] as translated by Joe Earle and the visual artistry of the gardens themselves as photographed by Sadao Hibi. *Infinite Spaces* offers us all a chance to partake of the art and wisdom of *Sakuteiki*. Let us look at the history of Japanese garden design to understand how the ideas set out in this ancient text have continued to exert their influence throughout the ages.

Religion and Garden Design

According to Japan's indigenous religion, Shinto, certain natural objects – mountains, hills, trees and stones – house divine spirits. Even today, a hiker in the forest might come upon a shrine area spread with white gravel and enclosed in simple bamboo or rope fencing. In the middle might stand a large stone called *iwakura*, which would be bound with ritual rice-straw rope, an indication of the presence of *kami*, or spirit guardians. The most famous of these sanctified spaces is the Ise shrine. For more than a thousand years, this holy site has housed thatched shrine buildings that are fully reconstructed every twenty years. An adjacent site stands ready for new buildings, and when these are completed a transferral ceremony is held and the old buildings are disassembled. Each vacant shrine site, standing in the pristine forest, suggests the belief in the sanctity of natural beauty that is at the heart of Japanese garden design.

During the Nara period (710–794), there was extensive cultural intercourse between Japan and Tang-dynasty China. In its gardens, architecture, legal systems, city design and even language, the island nation began to borrow from its more sophisticated continental neighbour. The symmetrical design of the garden of the Shishinden [Hall of the Screened Mansion], one of the great ceremonial buildings of the Kyoto Imperial Palace, suggests this growing Chinese influence: white gravel – like that at the Ise shrine – is spread in a courtyard between wooden buildings flanked by a mandarin orange tree and a cherry tree.

Stroll Gardens

Residential gardens of the Heian period (794–1185) were bright and relaxed spaces, featuring large ponds with islands for boating or viewing. Aristocrats such as Tachibana no Toshitsuna, the presumed author of *Sakuteiki*, occupied south-facing *shinden*-style mansions and employed *shoji* [rice-paper screens] and *tatami* [grass mats that covered the floor]. Pure Land Buddhism, which offered the hope of salvation and entrance into the Western Paradise after death, exerted a religious influence on garden design. Gardens of this period, whether residential or religious, often attempted to re-create the delights of the paradise offered by Amida Buddha. Ponds with tree-lined shores and rocky islands were the ideal, and sophisticated designs for bridges, waterfalls, streams and plantings, all discussed in *Sakuteiki*, developed as garden-making emerged as an art form that would reach its highest level in Japan's medieval age.

Some of the concepts introduced in *Sakuteiki* can be seen in the famous "Moss Temple", Saihoji, in the western hills of Kyoto. Said to have been created by the great Buddhist prelate Muso Kokushi (1275–1351), the garden was originally built in the earlier Pure Land lake-and-islands pattern, but was infused with a new religious spirit, that of Zen Buddhism, in 1339. Earlier gardens were designed to be seen from the interior of a building or from a boat on a pond, but at Saihoji the lower part of the four-and-a-half acre site is designed as a stroll garden, in which views of the landscape change as one walks through its spaces along tamped earth paths. Another and even more influential innovation may be seen in the upper garden, built on a rocky hillside to the north. Here large, lichen-covered stones seem to tumble down the hillside in a series of waterfalls and stepped pools. Yet no water ever actually circulated here. Muso Kokushi may have placed these stones as a powerful *karesansui* [dry landscape] composition, thought to be the first ever built for contemplation by the monks who inhabited the temple. Its abstract power has influenced the designers of *karesansui* gardens ever since.

Jojuin shrine, Kiyomizudera temple, Kyoto

Meditation Gardens

During the Muromachi period (1335–1573), small Zen gardens were built in which Zen monks tried many different approaches to the design of stone gardens in an attempt to convey the Zen concepts of discipline, self-examination and ultimate enlightenment. Often placed on the south-facing side of a Zen temple's prayer hall, *karesansui* meditation gardens featured white sand or gravel as the ground cover, raked in various patterns to suggest waves, droplets, ripples, or other effects. The garden of Daisen'in in Kyoto houses a miniature natural landscape, said to be a three-dimensional representation of the Chinese scroll paintings that influenced Zen thought at the time. Three sections of the garden, two of them less than ten feet in depth, hold stones arranged as a course of water falling over a waterfall, flowing through a mountain stream-bed, past a broad river and into a vast ocean, all indicated through stones and raked gravel. Other gardens are more abstract. The most famous of these is Ryoanji, a rectangular space about the size of a tennis court with five "islands" of moss and stone, comprising five, two, three, two and three rocks respectively, rising from a bed of raked gravel symbolizing the sea. While the composition as a whole is asymmetrical, balance is achieved through hierarchy. One's eyes and mind travel around the garden in a kind of circle, from the highest rocks to the lowest, giving the garden a sense of motion. From no point on the veranda can all fifteen rocks be seen at once: one rock is always hidden. Looking at the garden, one feels like the fifteenth rock, a part of the total composition. Soothed by the serene simplicity of the spare materials, one becomes an island, like Japan itself, floating upon a vast sea.

In time, new techniques were developed for creating the illusion of depth in a small space. One was the use of walls as a visual passage between the miniature landscape in the foreground and the larger landscape beyond. This method, called *shakkei* [borrowed landscape], makes tiny gardens appear much larger. The foreground may be a dry landscape of rocks, moss and small shrubs, behind which lies a carefully groomed hedge, with a grove of trees behind it. The trees are pruned so that only the tops have branches, leaving long slim trunks to suggest a natural frame. Enclosed by the hedge on the bottom, the trunks on the sides and the branches above, the distant view – such as a mountain – becomes part of the garden. The eye travels between two worlds, the miniature landscape in front and the distant mountainscape in the background, to create a dynamic balance through depth.

The Momoyama period (1574–1603) brought two new aesthetic ideals to Japanese gardens. The first was a gorgeous, opulent look that the military dictator Toyotomi Hideyoshi demanded in his architecture and gardens, with an abundance of colourful, powerful rocks, often stolen from courtiers and vanquished foes. At the same time, a reaction to his extravagance set in, and the restraint, refinement and dark simplicity of the tea ceremony became popular. Tea master Sen no Rikyu, Hideyoshi's aesthetic advisor, developed a style that infused gardens with a sense of impoverished elegance that influences garden-making even today.

Tea Gardens

The area that surrounds a tea house is called *roji*, literally "dewy path" or tea garden. Its purpose is to spiritually prepare visitors by leading them on a journey of stepping-stones, over thresholds, through gates and past lanterns, to a water basin where they purify hands and mouth before moving on to the tea house where the host serves powdered green tea in a ritualized ceremony.

Since a tea garden is designed to provide a series of spatial impressions in a tiny area, the design of its path is critical. *Tobiishi* [stepping-stones] are a constant motif, variously used. Small *tobiishi* placed next to each other slow the pace and direct the gaze downward, larger stones enable the guest to stop to look at some special view, and *nobedan* [long stone planks] allow the step to quicken in anticipation of the tea house around the bend. Each stone has a purpose, whether it be to focus the visitor upon the act of moving through the garden, to rid the mind of mundane thoughts, or to anticipate the quiet serenity of the tea ceremony. Tea gardens, despite their tiny dimensions, often have multiple paths, closed or open to entry by the placement of a single *yogoseki* [reed-bound rock] upon the initial stepping-stone. Detours from the path are brief, perhaps only to wash one's hands in a stone basin, and always the path provides the continuity that links the various parts of the garden experience.

Current Trends in Japanese Gardening

Modern Japanese gardens often combine the three major styles – the stroll garden, the meditation garden and the tea garden – and Western and Chinese features are increasingly being incorporated into Japanese design in the form of public and semi-public parks, institutional gardens and private residences. Despite its great antiquity, *Sakuteiki* remains a vital influence for garden-making in today's Japan. Enjoy Tachibana no Toshitsuna's words, delight in these exquisite photographs, and learn the secrets of Japanese garden design as you absorb the art and wisdom contained in *Infinite Spaces*.

A Note on *Sakuteiki*

Joe Earle

We know very little about the origins of *Sakuteiki* [Notes on Garden Design] beyond the fact that it was already in existence by the year 1289, when a calligrapher called Kujo Yoshitsune inscribed his name at the end of the oldest surviving copy of the work. Most Japanese scholars agree, however, that *Sakuteiki* was written about a century earlier by Tachibana no Toshitsuna (1028–94), also known as Fujiwara no Toshitsuna. He was a poet and courtier, supposedly the son of Tachibana no Shun'en but more probably the son of Fujiwara no Yorimichi, one of the most important figures in eleventh-century Japan. At the age of fifteen (not unusual in those days), Toshitsuna was made a provincial governor. He is said to have been a virtuous administrator and was eventually awarded a sinecure at court, spending much of his time, it seems, pursuing his passion for garden design on his estate in the Fushimi hills to the south of the capital, Kyoto.

Toshitsuna's presumed father Yorimichi was the head of the Fujiwara family of Regents, and it was Yorimichi's father Michinaga (966–1027) who had brought the power of that great clan to its peak by marrying his daughters into the Japanese Imperial family: towards the end of his life Michinaga could boast that three Emperors were his sons-in-law and four were his grandsons. By the time that *Sakuteiki* was written, however, a decline had set in, not only in the prestige of the Fujiwara but also in the power and even the relevance of the entire system of government they headed. Although Yorimichi was appointed Regent in 1019 and exercised this office for over half a century, his daughter, also married into the Imperial family, failed to produce a male heir. Away from Kyoto, military leadership was passing into the hands of warlike regional clans that would, in time, seize control of the entire country and burn much of the capital to the ground.

Whether or not Toshitsuna was actually the son of Yorimichi, he and his aristocratic friends would have shared a strong sense that the golden age of the Fujiwara was coming to an end. The same feeling of nostalgia that pervades Japan's greatest novel, *Genji monogatari* [The Tale of Genji] completed by Lady Murasaki Shikibu not long before Toshitsuna's birth, is expressed by the author of *Sakuteiki* when he laments characteristically that "These days there is no one left who really understands gardening". *Sakuteiki* tells us that when Toshitsuna's father Yorimichi wanted to restore the Kayanoin palace, it was already impossible to find artisans who were skilled in building gardens, so that in the end Yorimichi himself was forced to oversee the work. It was then, perhaps, that Toshitsuna gained his early experience of garden art.

Sakuteiki is best understood as an attempt to preserve the accumulated practical experience of centuries of garden design, illuminated by the author's elite knowledge of Chinese and Japanese literature and belief. The original text runs to over 12,000 characters and this is no more than a partial rendering in a contemporary idiom intended to appeal to gardeners rather than historians. Few modern enthusiasts are likely to be interested in building an exact recreation of an eleventh-century Kyoto garden in the Western Paradise style mentioned by Julie Moir Messervy, not least because the average plot size for an aristocrat's residence was an entire block, measuring about 400 by 400 feet. While many gardens today include ponds and other water features, they are unlikely to be big enough for islands which can accommodate a "music pavilion up to seventy or eighty feet square". There is much along these grandiose lines in *Sakuteiki* and I have excluded almost everything that is too closely related to the specific circumstances of eleventh-century Kyoto. It should also be pointed out that Toshitsuna regarded gardening as mainly a matter of landscaping. He has very little to say about plants (other than trees) and since the few remarks he does make apply to very specific design situations these too have been omitted.

Sakuteiki starts off with an exposition of general principles and continues with practical advice on different features, but thereafter it jumps bewilderingly from subject to subject, with a mixture of detailed categorizations, historical anecdotes and lists of taboos and prohibitions. For this reason it was decided to rearrange the text under headings that would appeal to modern gardeners and complement Sadao Hibi's superb photographs. The extraordinary thing is that so much of this nine-hundred-year-old text fits perfectly with images of later Japanese gardens and is also in tune with garden design as it is practised around the world today. The belief in our capacity to improve on nature at the same time as respecting its innate qualities, the insistence on adhering to general principles rather than detailed rules, even the interest in the complex of Chinese beliefs and auspicious practices that we now call Feng shui – all these aspects of *Sakuteiki* continue to strike a chord in the twenty-first century. Above all we should heed Toshitsuna's advice on the importance of "secret teaching", meaning (I suspect) the kind of teaching that cannot be set down in words but can only be learned through experience. The best way to use *Sakuteiki* is to get out into your garden and put its ideas into practice.

Next page: Saihoji temple (the 'Moss Temple'), Kyoto

作庭記

Chapter 1

Principles of
Garden Design

Previous page:

Shimotokikuni family garden, Ishikawa

"Always remember to make the style suit the site."

Oyakuen, Iwate

"These days there is no one left who really understands gardening. They just look at natural landscapes and then go ahead with their design without observing the many important taboos that have to be observed."

Momijidani garden, Wakayama

"We should always remember that it is not practical for ordinary people to live in the depths of the mountains.

So how can it be wrong for them to build waterfalls by their hillside cottages and plant a few trees as well? Pay no attention to anyone who tells you that you must not plant trees in this or that place!"

Previous page: Oyakuen garden, Iwate

Moroto family garden, Mie

"It has been said that stones arranged by man can never be better than a natural landscape. But in my extensive travels around the country I can remember several occasions when I have been struck by the beauty of a particular spot, only to find that the adjoining scenery is quite unremarkable."

"Take your inspiration from the masterpieces of the great designers of the past, but keep your client's wishes in mind and make sure that the garden is also an expression of your own personal vision."

"Think of the finest natural landscapes you have seen, select those that you find most inspiring and adapt them to your plan, copying their overall features and making them blend in with your chosen site."

名所

"The painter and gardener Hirotaka taught that stones should never be placed carelessly."

Kyugetsutei pavilion, Shiga

"Because it is difficult to appreciate an arrangement at close quarters you should always try to make sure that your design will look best when viewed at a short distance."

"When you design your garden you can pick and choose from the very best that you have seen in nature, ensuring that every stone contributes something to the overall effect."

"It is sometimes said that landscape designs and arrangements of stones carry deeper, hidden, meanings. For example, the earth can symbolize the ruler and the water his subjects. Water can only go where the earth allows it and must come to a halt where the earth obstructs it.

According to one theory, the mound symbolizes the ruler, the earth his subjects and the water his ministers. In this analogy the water flows where the mound dictates, but if the mound is unstable it will be washed away by the water, symbolizing a weak ruler being deposed by his subjects. If the mound is unstable it is because there are no stones supporting it, and if a ruler is weak it is because he has no ministers. A mound is made complete by stones just as a ruler is protected by his ministers. This goes to show what an important contribution stones can make to a successful landscape design."

Eihoji temple, Gifu

"Make sure that
your design
harmonizes with
the lie of the
land, the shape
of the pond
and any other
existing features.
As you set out
your garden,
never forget how
the site looked in
its natural state."

風情

Previous page: Eihoji temple, Gifu

Jizoin shrine, Mie

"When you are making up your mind how many stones to use and where to place them, be guided by the lie of the land as well as your own passing mood."

Koetsuji temple, Kyoto

"It makes me laugh when ignorant visitors insist on being told the specific 'style' of every garden they see!"

Next page:
Saiokuji temple, Shizuoka

Pools and Lakes

Kannon'in shrine, Tottori

"Ponds should always be shallow.
Deep ponds allow the fish to grow
too big and turn into poisonous bugs."

Enman'in shrine, Shiga

"When you plan to dig a pond and set out your stones, first take a careful look at the
lie of the land. In shaping your pond, building islands and deciding where the water
should flow in and out, work in harmony with the environment."

Sento Gosho palace, Kyoto

Myoganji temple, Aichi

"It should be impossible to see where the water goes in and out. Keep the inlets hidden, and ensure that the pond is filled to the brim."

"Water takes its shape from the container into which it flows, with both good and bad results. Therefore you should always exercise the greatest care with the design of your ponds."

"When you are designing the islands for your garden, be sure to take into account both the appearance of the surrounding land and the size of the pond."

Previous page:

Aizu Matsudaira family garden, Fukushima

Sakai family garden, Yamagata

Former Yasuda family garden, Tokyo

"Your ponds and conduits should be laid out so that the water flows towards the south-west, helping to carry inauspicious influences from the direction of the Blue Dragon in the east to that of the White Tiger in the west."

Tenshaen garden, Ehime

"If you have a large pond with islands in it, you should try to make the pond look like the sea, while the rest of the garden should be landscaped and planted to resemble a piece of calligraphy."

Suizenji Jojuen park, Kumamoto

Kenrokuen garden, Ishikawa

"To create the effect of a wild seacoast, start by scattering a few rough, pointed rocks along the shore of your pond. Then place lines of rocks out into the water, so that they look as if they have just grown from the bottom of the pond. There should also be a few isolated rocks still further away from the shore."

Koishikawa Korakuen garden, Tokyo

Next page: Chishakuin shrine, Kyoto

Enshoji temple, Fukui

滝を立る事

Chapter 3

Waterfalls

Erinji temple, Yamanashi

"Fudo, the Implacable Guardian King of Buddhism, once swore that waterfalls three feet high or more were symbols of his physical body, still more so if they were as much as ten or twenty feet in height. Waterfalls as tall as this always take the form of the Buddhist trinity of Fudo with two attendants, symbolized by two smaller stones standing at the foot of the main vertical stone. The holy scriptures state:

He who sees my body shall attain enlightenment. He who hears my words shall learn to reject evil and practise good... That is why they call me 'Implacable'...

Among the many forms taken by Fudo the Implacable, the waterfall most truly reveals his true nature."

"When laying out the area below the waterfall, start by placing two well-shaped stones at the left and right, each of them about half the height of the larger rocks framing the cascade, then place smaller stones downstream in a way that suits the mood of the first two stones.

For best results, make the area below the waterfall as wide as possible and place plenty of stones in the middle of the water so that the stream is divided in two. After that, you can lay out the stream just as you would for an ordinary water feature."

Chishakuin shrine, Kyoto

Mori family garden, Yamaguchi

"A stream can be made to descend a waterfall in several different ways. In the *Facing* style, there should be two elegantly shaped cascades falling side by side. In the *One-Sided* style the cascade falls down the left hand side of the vertical stone. In front and to the left of the vertical stone, place another stone about half its size, and shape this stone so that when the cascade falls onto it, the water whitens and drops to the right. In the *Following* style the water falls down along the cracks in the surface of the vertical stone. For the *Separated* style, on top of the vertical stone place another stone with a well-defined angle along one edge in such a way that it does not obstruct the flow of water. The water passes swiftly over the edge and falls down without actually touching the face of the vertical stone. In the *Corner* style the top of the waterfall is tilted to one side so that it is seen to good effect when viewed from the best room in your house. To create a waterfall in the *Cloth* style you need to find a really well-formed vertical stone and then shape the stream above the cascade so that the water slows down and drops gently over the edge; the waterfall will then look like a piece of cloth that has been hung out to air. For the *Threads* style, on top of the vertical stone place another stone with a jagged, irregular edge which will divide the water into several little thread-like cascades. For the *Compound* style set up two vertical stones and without trying anything too elaborate just let the water fall down in two or three steps."

Nijo castle, Kyoto

月に向ふべきなり

"It is sometimes said that you should try to manipulate your waterfall so that the falling sheet of water reflects the light of the moon. I expect there is a secret teaching about this, or you could probably learn a lot from Chinese gardening books!"

"It is sometimes said that you should not build waterfalls in places that are dark and overhung by trees. This advice can be safely ignored. In fact waterfalls that descend from tree-darkened ravines are particularly good to look at, although all the examples I have seen are in old gardens."

Erinji temple, Yamanashi

"If you look at natural waterfalls, you will notice that high waterfalls are not always wide, and low waterfalls are not always narrow. The only thing that makes any difference is the width of the lip over which the water actually flows. All the same, a waterfall three or four feet high should not be more than about two feet wide.

A low, wide waterfall is unsatisfactory in several respects. It can look very flat or even be mistaken for a dam, and if the point where the water falls over the rock is fully visible, the whole scene will lack depth."

遣水の石を立る事

Negoroji temple, Wakayama

Previous page:

Senshukaku pavilion, Tokushima castle, Tokushima

Kongorinji temple, Shiga

"When you place a lot of stones at a point where the stream makes a turn, they may seem just right if you are next to them but look surprisingly artificial when you view them from a few paces away."

"To create the effect of a river landscape, shape the stream like the meandering trail left by a dragon or snake. Decide where you want the stream to turn a corner, then choose a really well-shaped stone and place it there. Everything else you do in the garden should be dictated by this first stone. There is a secret teaching about this!"

Motsuji temple, Iwate

"No matter where a stream flows from, it should be interesting to look at without necessarily being in the latest fashion. Dig the channel so that the stream flows this way and that, passing first one hillside and then another as the landscape dictates."

"When setting the gradient for your garden streams, the ratio of height to distance should be three in one hundred: this makes the water flow along smoothly with a gentle murmur. But in the lower reaches, where the landscape is gentler, the water will be pushed along by the faster water upstream."

Kenrokuen garden, Ishikawa

Nijo castle, Kyoto

"When laying out a stream, never pack stones tightly together in places where they will easily catch the viewer's attention. Instead, groups of stones should be positioned where the stream emerges from under your house, where it goes round the side of a mound, where it flows into the pond or where it makes a sharp bend.

Start by putting one stone at each of these points and then add as many or as few other stones as the first stone dictates."

遣水

Murin'an sub-temple. Kyoto

Fumon'in shrine, Koyasan temple complex, Wakayama

"When arranging the stones for a stream, start by concentrating on points where the stream makes a sharp bend. Make it look as though there was always a stone at each bend and the water was forced to turn a corner because it could not wash the stone away.

After the stream has turned it will flow with extra momentum and strike hard against the next obstacle it encounters. Wherever it looks as though this is going to happen, install a 'turning-stone', doing the same for each subsequent bend in the stream. Elsewhere, place stones here and there in the stream as you think fit, but make them look as if they had almost been left there by accident."

"Every home should have a spring. There is nowhere better to escape the summer heat."

The former Shurinji temple, Shiga

泉

Motsuji temple, Iwate

大海様

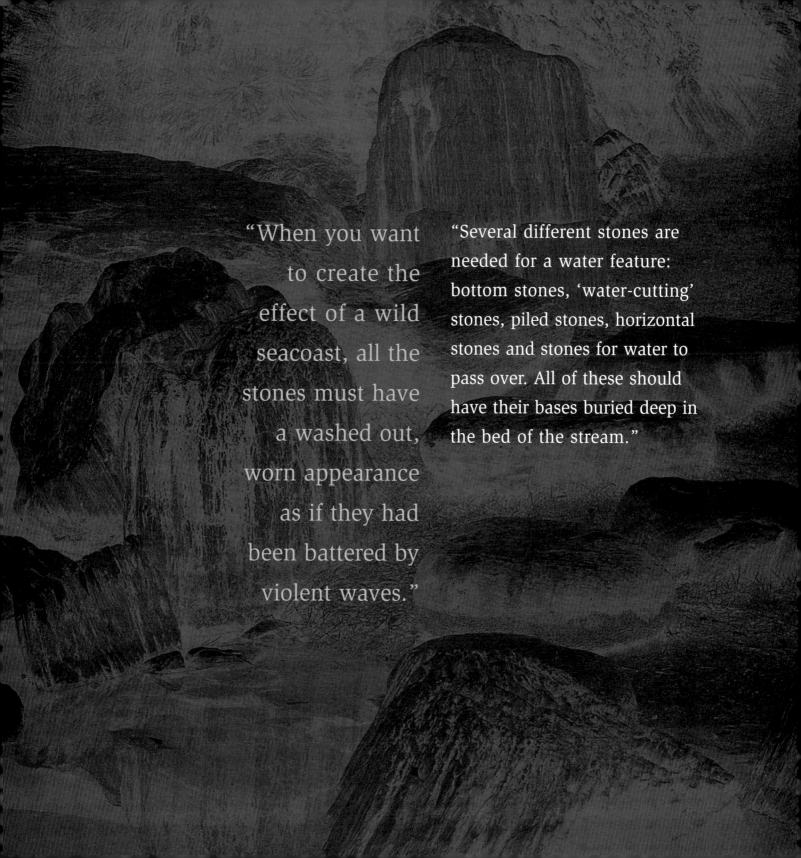

"When you want to create the effect of a wild seacoast, all the stones must have a washed out, worn appearance as if they had been battered by violent waves."

"Several different stones are needed for a water feature: bottom stones, 'water-cutting' stones, piled stones, horizontal stones and stones for water to pass over. All of these should have their bases buried deep in the bed of the stream."

Saimyoji temple, Shiga

Negoroji temple, Wakayama

Chapter 5

Trees and Mounds

Saihoji temple (the 'Moss Temple'), Kyoto

73

Previous page:

Jishoji temple (the 'Silver Pavilion'), Kyoto

Tenryuji temple, Kyoto

"As you lay out your garden, always remember to keep your overall plan in mind."

Koishikawa Korakuen garden, Tokyo

"When the Buddha preached he stood under a tree. When the Shinto gods come down from heaven they take up residence in trees. So is it not essential that human habitations should be surrounded by trees?"

"Apart from the special trees symbolizing the Four Cardinal Points you can plant trees wherever you like. However, it is worth knowing that people used to say that trees grown for their flowers should be planted on the east side of your garden, while trees grown for their foliage should be planted on the west side."

Momijidani garden, Wakayama

"Planting a tree creates an earthly paradise."

凡樹は人中天上の荘厳也

"How to plant trees around your house to ensure that the Four Cardinal Points are effectively symbolized:

An ancient Chinese text states that a stream flowing from the house towards the east symbolizes the Blue Dragon. If there is no stream, plant nine willow trees instead.

A wide path to the west of the house symbolizes the White Tiger. If there is no such path, plant seven catalpas instead.

A pond to the south of the house symbolizes the Red Bird. If there is no pond, plant nine Judas trees instead.

A mound to the north of the house symbolizes the Dark Warrior. If there is no mound, plant three cypress trees instead."

Kenrokuen, Ishikawa   Next page: Suizenji Jojuen park, Kumamoto

"To capture the mood of a mountain village or some other attractive country spot, build a tall mound of earth near your house and arrange a few rocks so that they appear to be flowing down from the summit to the base."

"When the Chinese Emperor Qinshi Huangdi burnt all the books and buried the scholars alive, he issued a special decree exempting books on the cultivation of trees."

禁忌

Chapter 6

Good and Evil

Garden in the remains of the
Kitabatake family residence, Mie

"Before you do anything else, decide where you want your stream to begin. According to the ancient Chinese texts, the water in a garden should normally flow from the east, first in a southerly direction and then towards the west...It is best of all if the water starts in the east, passes underneath your house and then flows towards the south-west, taking water from the Blue Dragon in the east and flushing all evil influences away towards the White Tiger in the west. A household where this rule is observed will be free of epidemics and diseases of the skin, and its occupants will live long and peaceful lives...But if the stream has to start from the north it should turn east before flowing on towards the south-west."

Shotoen garden, Fukuoka

身心安寿命長遠

Kongorinji temple, Shiga

Saiokuji temple, Shizuoka

Natadera temple, Ishikawa

Rikugien garden, Tokyo

Next page: Shimotokikuni family garden, Ishikawa

弘法大師高野山に至りて

"The great priest Kukai, the founder of the Shingon sect of Buddhism, went in search of the finest scenery in Japan and visited Mount Koya, where he met the guardian spirit of the place disguised as an old man. When Kukai asked him if there was anywhere on the mountain that might make a suitable site for a temple, the old man replied 'Within this domain of mine there is a place where purple clouds hang in the sky by day, where the five-needled pine emanates an auspicious glow by night and where all the waters flow towards the east. Such a place would be perfect even for a mighty castle.'

This might seem to contradict the teaching that water should flow towards the west, but in this case the eastward flow of the water symbolized the eastward spread of the Buddha's teaching. One need not follow this example when deciding how to lay out a house and its garden."

"Flat stones should never be set so that they point towards the north-west. If you break this rule, you will never grow rich."

"I have found that stones inhabited by vengeful spirits always land the right way up if they fall from a height. Such stones should not be used. Throw them away!"

"Some Chinese texts claim that the waters in a garden should flow from north to south. Since the north symbolizes water and the south symbolizes fire, maybe this saying should be taken to mean that if you make the water flow from north to south you will bring yin from the north and harmonize it with yang in the south."

"According to the ancient Chinese texts, the inner side of the curve of a stream symbolizes the belly of a dragon. It is auspicious if your house is located within the curve, but unlucky if it is located on the outside of the curve."

Gyokusenji temple, Yamagata

石を立る事

Chapter 7

Stones

Shinnyoin shrine, Kyoto

"There should
always be more
horizontal than
vertical stones."

Senshukaku pavilion, Tokushima

"When you start work on your garden, have a selection of different-sized stones delivered and laid out on the ground so that you can see the tops of the standing stones and the upper surfaces of the lying stones. Then it will be easy for you to match and compare them, selecting stones one at a time as your design takes shape."

"Stones can be arranged around some garden feature, for example the bottom of a hill, the foot of a tree or a pillar of your house."

Nagoya castle, Aichi

Next page: Kozenji temple, Nagano

宋人云

A Chinese commentator remarked *"Stones that are found lying on a steep hillside or at the valley bottom sometimes come to rest the wrong way up after they have crumbled away from the tops of mountains or the sides of rivers. As the years go by they will change colour and moss will grow on them. This process is quite natural, so when you use such stones in your garden you should not hesitate to place them as you found them, even though they were originally in a different position."*

Seishuraigoji temple, Shiga

Joeiji temple, Yamaguchi

"Stones at the bottom of a hill where it meets the plain should look like dogs crouching on the ground, pigs running around, or a calf playing near its mother."

Saioin shrine, Kyoto

"If there are 'running away' stones there must be 'chasing' stones.

If there are 'leaning' stones there must be 'supporting' stones.

If there are 'assertive' stones there must be 'yielding' stones.

If there are 'upward-looking' stones there must be 'downward-looking' stones.

If there are 'vertical' stones there must be 'horizontal' stones."

石の乞んに従ひて立るなり

Ryoanji temple, Kyoto

Hokokuji temple, Ehime

Ryoanji temple, Kyoto

枯山水

"When you build a *karesansui* [dry landscape] garden, you should first model the whole site to look like the base of a mountain or a hillside field, then arrange the stones so that they fit in with your overall design."

"Gardens can be built in places where there are no ponds or streams. Such gardens are referred to as *karesansui*."

Jishoji temple (the 'Silver Pavilion'), Kyoto

臥る石に立てる石
のなきは苦みなし

"Try not to place tall stones on either side of waterfalls,
in front of islands or at the foot of mounds."

Fukada family garden, Tottori

"It is not a problem if a lying stone does not have a standing stone next to it, but a standing stone must have accompanying stones to left and right, and the foremost standing stone in an arrangement must have a lying stone next to it. It looks stupid when standing stones, without horizontal stones, are laid out in rows like the rivets on a helmet!"

Tenjuan sub-temple, Kyoto

Shinnyoin shrine, Kyoto

Shoryakuji temple, Nara

"Stones should be set securely in place with their bases deep in the ground. Even so a second stone can be leant against a securely placed stone in such a way that the first stone looks insecure, and vice versa. There is a secret teaching about this!"

"Make sure that all the stones, right down to the one at the front of the arrangement, are placed with their best sides showing. If a stone has an ugly-looking top you should place it so as to give prominence to its side. Even if this means it has to lean at a considerable angle, no one will notice."

Daitokuji temple, Kyoto

"Create your foreground design by combining a suitably-shaped principal stone with two smaller stones to its left and right. The arrangement of the stones in the background should be dictated by the needs of the principal stone."

"Always begin by positioning a particularly well-shaped stone and let it dictate the arrangement of all the other stones."

Seishuraigoji temple, Shiga

"Although I have managed to get hold of several treatises on gardening and learn the basic principles of garden design, I have come to realise that there are almost endless possibilities, including many that are far too profound for me."

予又その文書を伝へ得たり。如此相営みて、大旨を心得たりと雖も、風情尽ることなくして、心及ばざること多し。